PEOPLE AT
THE CENTER OF

WOMEN'S SUFFRAGE

By DEBORAH KOPS

BLACKBIRCH™
PRESS

THOMSON
───✦───
GALE

San Diego • Detroit • New York • San Francisco • Cleveland
New Haven, Conn. • Waterville, Maine • London • Munich

THOMSON
✳
GALE

For more information, contact
The Gale Group, Inc.
27500 Drake Rd.
Farmington Hills, MI 48331-3535
Or you can visit our Internet site at http://www.gale.com

LIBRARY OF CONGRESS CATALOGING-IN-PUBLICATION DATA

Kops, Deborah.
  The women suffrage movement / By Deborah Kops.
    p. cm. — (People at the center of:)
  Summary: Profiles early leaders in the fight for women's rights, especially the right to
vote, including Mary Wollstonecraft, Lucretia Mott, Sojourner Truth, and Elizabeth Cady
Stanton.
  Includes bibliographical references and index.
  ISBN 1-56711-772-4 (alk. paper)
  1. Suffragists—United States—Biography—Juvenile literature. 2. Women—Suffrage—
United States—History—Juvenile literature. [1. Suffragists. 2. Women—Suffrage. 3.
Women's rights. 4. Women—Biography.] I. Title. II. Series.
  JK1898.K67 2004
  324.6'23'092273—dc21   2003007099

Printed in United States
10 9 8 7 6 5 4 3 2 1

CONTENTS

PEOPLE AT
THE CENTER OF

THE WOMEN'S SUFFRAGE MOVEMENT

On August 18, 1920, members of Tennessee's legislature gathered in Nashville for a special session. They were going to vote on the proposed Nineteenth Amendment to the Constitution, which would give women the right to vote.

With a touch of drama, legislators who opposed the amendment wore red roses, and supporters wore yellow ones. The suffragists realized they were short one vote, and they were not sure where it would come from. When Harry Burns's name was called, many assumed he would vote against the amendment because he was wearing a red rose. In Burns's pocket, however, was a note from his elderly mother instructing him to vote for suffrage. Apparently, he was an obedient son. When he voted for the amendment, the suffragists in the balcony erupted in cheers. Twenty-six million women in the United States had just won the right to vote.

The women's suffrage movement—women's struggle for the right to vote— extended over a very long period of U.S. history. The seeds of the movement began to take root around the 1830s, when many women participated in the large reform movements sweeping the country. For example, some joined temperance societies to encourage men to pledge not to drink because they thought that alcoholism was becoming a national problem. Many women in the North belonged to antislavery groups and tried to bring an end to slavery.

Women became more politically active in the nineteenth century. Their participation in various social causes culminated in the women's suffrage movement.

When the earliest of these reformers gave public lectures to encourage men and women to join their cause, they were scolded for being unladylike. Frustrated with the limitations society imposed on their sex, they began to give talks on women's rights as well as on slavery. Other women followed in their footsteps, and their public protests became the beginning of the women's suffrage movement.

Above: Both men and women attended the first women's rights convention at the Wesleyan Chapel in Seneca Falls, New York. Opposite: Elizabeth Cady Stanton, depicted here as she speaks at a convention, cofounded the National Woman Suffrage Association.

In 1848, Elizabeth Cady Stanton and Lucretia Mott organized a women's rights convention with the hope of improving the status of American women. At the convention, which took place in Seneca Falls, New York, on July 19 and 20, Stanton proposed a resolution for women's suffrage, or voting rights. The idea that women were entitled to vote was revolutionary: Most Americans believed that a husband or father should be a family's representative at the voting poll. Eloquently supported by the great African American antislavery leader Frederick Douglass, the resolution was approved by a majority of the three hundred women and men who attended that historic meeting. It was the first organized demand for women's suffrage anywhere in the world. During the next decade, many women's rights conventions were organized in almost every region of the United States.

After the Civil War (1861–1865), the suffragists, who numbered in the thousands, disagreed over whether to support the Fifteenth Amendment to the Constitution. It gave the vote to black men but not to women, regardless of their race. The two suffragist leaders who had become symbols of the movement, Elizabeth Cady Stanton and her good friend and partner in the struggle, Susan B. Anthony, opposed the Fifteenth Amendment. They had hoped that after the war, all American citizens, blacks and whites, would be able to vote. They felt betrayed by their old antislavery and Republican friends, who seemed to be deserting the women's suffrage cause. In 1869, Stanton and Anthony formed a new organization, the National Woman Suffrage Association (NWSA), and campaigned for a constitutional amendment to give women the vote. Lucy Stone, a more moderate suffrage leader from Massachusetts who supported the Fifteenth Amendment, helped establish a second group, the American Woman Suffrage Association, which focused on winning votes for women state by state. That same year, the territory of Wyoming became the first territory or state to grant women the right to vote in all elections. Utah followed in 1870.

During the twenty-one years that the two organizations worked separately, the women's suffrage movement grew into a larger movement with deeper roots. Women's suffrage societies sprouted all over the country. When the Women's Christian Temperance Union decided to support women's right to vote, thousands of its members joined the cause.

In 1890, Stanton, Anthony, and Stone, urged by a younger generation of suffragists, finally united their two organizations to form the new National American Woman Suffrage Association (NAWSA). The new organization did not produce any dramatic changes during the next two decades. Only two more states gave women the vote—Idaho and Colorado. Many thought the suffrage movement was in the doldrums, but not for long.

By 1912 the suffrage movement was once again lively, vigorous, and filled with hope. A new reform movement, called the Progressive movement, was winning supporters in both parties. The women who worked for these reforms, such as better working conditions for factory workers and an end to child labor, realized that they would be more effective if they could vote. Many joined the ranks of the suffragists.

In addition to the Progressives, two women in particular helped breathe new life into the struggle—Alice Paul and Carrie Catt. They pursued entirely different strategies. Alice Paul and her radical National Woman's Party used aggressive, attention-getting tactics that got a lot of people talking about suffrage again. Carrie Catt, who became president of NAWSA in 1915, took a more moderate approach.

In 1916, NAWSA tried to boost the number of states with women's suffrage, which stood at ten. At the same time, the organization conducted a massive effort to persuade Congress and

Opposite: In the early 1900s, some leaders of the suffrage movement used more visible forms of publicity, and suffragist ranks grew. Above: Carrie Catt (center) and another suffrage leader voted for the first time in 1920.

President Woodrow Wilson to pass a national amendment. The results were three state victories, including New York, and a convert in the White House. When Wilson instructed Congress to pass the women's suffrage amendment, which had been voted down every year since 1878, they cooperated. The Nineteenth Amendment to the Constitution was passed in June 1919. Thirty-six state legislatures had to ratify it before it became law. The Tennessee legislature cast the decisive thirty-sixth vote in 1920.

Suffragists celebrated the ratification of the Nineteenth Amendment, which gave women the right to vote.

Margaret Brent was born in Gloucester, England, in 1601. Her family was financially well-off and very large. One of thirteen children, she learned about managing a large property by watching the activities of her father, Richard. Brent's family was Catholic, and in the mid-1600s Catholics were persecuted by the Protestant majority. Brent and some of her brothers and sisters decided to seek their fortunes in the colony of Maryland, which was established as a haven for Catholics by the powerful George Calvert, Lord Baltimore, an acquaintance of the family. They arrived on November 22, 1638.

Brent became very influential in the young colony, with some assistance from Governor Leonard Calvert, who was Lord Baltimore's brother. She soon became one of the largest landowners in Maryland. In 1648, when the governor lay dying, he asked Brent to be his executor and handle the affairs of his estate.

Brent was in a position to solve a continuing crisis that was threatening Maryland. The colony's capital, Saint Marys City, was overrun with unhappy soldiers from Virginia who demanded food and payment for their assistance in putting down a rebellion that had threatened Maryland. After the governor died, Brent sold his estate and some cattle that belonged to Lord Baltimore to feed and pay the soldiers, and she restored peace to the colony. It was a remarkable performance for a woman at a time when men completely dominated public life.

George Calvert,
Lord Baltimore

Next, Brent astonished the members of the assembly, where the people's representatives met, by demanding two votes. One vote was for herself, because she was a landowner, and the other was for the estate of Lord Baltimore, which she represented. Her audacious move earned her a place in history as the first American woman to demand the right to vote.

The House of Burgesses turned Brent down, and she soon moved on to the colony of Virginia, where she prospered again. She died about 1670.

Margaret Brent, a wealthy and influential landowner in Maryland, demanded the right to vote in 1648.

Mary Wollstonecraft was born near London in 1758. Her father dominated the family, and she grew up with a sense that girls and women had little control over their lives.

Wollstonecraft began writing books at the age of twenty-nine. Her first was a collection of essays on raising girls called *Thoughts on the Education of Daughters*, published in 1787. A novel and short stories followed. Her most important work, *The Vindication of the Rights of Woman*, was published in 1792.

Wollstonecraft presented a number of radical ideas in *The Vindication of the Rights of Woman*. She suggested that allowing women to vote would be good for society. Women were the spiritual equals of men, she claimed, and in marriage should be treated as partners. Wollstonecraft poked fun at those who thought of women as weak and shallow. A woman's education, she wrote, should prepare her to be a man's intellectual equal. Professions, such as the law, she thought, should be open

Left: Mary Wollstonecraft expressed her feminist views in writings that would later inspire key suffragist leaders. Above: A copy of Wollstonecraft's **The Vindication of the Rights of Woman.**

to women as well as men. Almost a century later, the two women who led the early years of the American women's suffrage movement, Elizabeth Cady Stanton and Susan B. Anthony, claimed that Wollstonecraft was one of their greatest inspirations.

In 1797, Wollstonecraft married William Godwin. She died later that year on September 10, soon after their daughter Mary was born. Mary became famous in her own right as the author of the horror novel *Frankenstein*, which she wrote under her married name, Mary Shelley.

Sarah and Angelina Grimké belonged to a large and prominent family in Charleston, South Carolina. Sarah, born on November 26, 1792, was the sixth of fourteen children. Angelina, born on February 20, 1805, was the youngest. The Grimkés kept scores of slaves, which troubled the girls. As an adult, Angelina joined the antislavery cause first. In 1836, she accepted a position with the American Anti-Slavery Society to speak to groups of women in New York City. Hundreds came to hear this eloquent Southerner denounce slavery. That summer, Sarah moved from her home in Philadelphia to New York to join her sister in the struggle.

Sarah (above) and Angelina (opposite) Grimké were vocal abolitionists whose demands for the equal treatment of women paved the way for suffragists.

In 1837, Angelina and Sarah went on a lecture tour of New England to speak out against slavery. Angelina did most of the speaking, often before large crowds of men and women. Her powerful voice and passionate conviction reached all the way to the back of the Boston Opera House, where she appeared six nights in a row. Her speeches unleashed a storm of protest from proper New Englanders. Men of the church, in particular, criticized Angelina for giving public addresses before mixed audiences of men and women. Suddenly the sisters were thrust into an argument over whether women had the right to voice their views publicly.

Although it pained the Grimkés, who were religious, to argue with the clergy, they did not back down. They wrote pamphlets in support of a woman's right to participate equally with men in the abolitionist movement, the most important reform movement of the day. They even suggested that women ought to be able to influence the laws of the nation directly. In speaking publicly and insisting on their right to do so, Angelina and Sarah paved the way for other women who followed.

In 1838, Angelina married the well-known abolitionist Theodore Weld. Sarah joined the couple in New Jersey and helped Angelina raise the Weld's three sons. Sarah died on December 23, 1873, when she was eighty-one. Angelina died on October 26, 1879, at the age of seventy-four.

LUCRETIA MOTT

Lucretia Coffin Mott grew up in a world that was unusually supportive of women. She was born on January 3, 1793, on the island of Nantucket in Massachusetts. There, women often managed business affairs while many of the men, like Lucretia's sea captain father, were away on voyages.

When she was eighteen, Lucretia married James Mott, a fellow Quaker. Six years later, in 1817, she became a minister. Like other Quakers, Mott opposed slavery, and she began to give speeches in support of its complete abolition. She was a delegate to the 1840 World Anti-Slavery Convention in London, but because she was a woman, she was forced to sit with visitors instead of other delegates. It was obvious to her and to a young American she befriended there, Elizabeth Cady Stanton, that women needed to fight for their own rights as well the rights of African Americans.

In 1848, on a visit to upstate New York, Mott met with her younger sister, Stanton, and three other women. They decided to hold a convention in a chapel in the nearby town of Seneca Falls to discuss the social, legal, and religious rights of women.

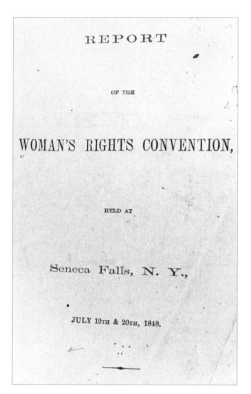

REPORT

OF THE

WOMAN'S RIGHTS CONVENTION,

HELD AT

Seneca Falls, N. Y.,

JULY 19TH & 20TH, 1848.

Opposite: Lucretia Mott spoke out for women's rights as well as the rights of African Americans. Above: Mott delivered the opening and closing addresses at the Seneca Falls Convention.

About 260 women and 40 men attended the Seneca Falls Convention, which began on July 19, 1848. Mott gave the opening and closing addresses. Among the resolutions passed at the convention was one on women's right to vote. Mott felt it was too soon to present such a revolutionary idea to the public, but Stanton insisted.

After the convention, Mott continued to speak out for women's rights, women's suffrage, and for the abolition of slavery. She died on January 26, 1868.

SOJOURNER TRUTH

FOUGHT FOR THE RIGHTS OF BOTH BLACK AND WHITE WOMEN

Born in 1797, Sojourner Truth was the daughter of slaves kept by a wealthy Dutch landowner in Ulster County, New York. Her parents named her Isabella. Two of her daughters were sold into slavery, but she was able to raise a third daughter and her son after New York State emancipated slaves there in 1827.

In 1843, Isabella took the name Sojourner Truth, and set out to become a traveling preacher. In Massachusetts, she discovered the antislavery movement and lent her great gifts as a speaker to that cause. She also spoke on behalf of women's rights. Large crowds of people attended her addresses, drawn by the wit, practical wisdom, and magnetic personality of this former slave who could neither read nor write.

In 1851, Sojourner Truth gave an unforgettable speech before a women's rights convention in Akron, Ohio. A group of clergymen had been heckling the women speakers, and one of them gave an antisuffrage talk. She pointed a long, bony finger at him and said:

> The man over there says women need to be helped into carriages and lifted over ditches. . . . Nobody ever helps me over puddles, or gives me the best place—and ain't I a woman? . . . Look at my arm! I have ploughed and planted and gathered into barns, and no man could head me—and ain't I a woman? I could work as much and eat as much as a man—when I could get it—and bear the lash as well! And ain't I a woman?

Sojourner Truth's speech is one of the most frequently quoted from the history of the suffrage movement, and it helped to make her a legend in her time. She was a living example of the importance that suffrage held for black women as well as white women.

In 1875, when her grandson and constant companion became ill, Sojourner Truth ended her lecture tours and settled down in Battle Creek, Michigan, where her three daughters lived. She died on November 26, 1883.

Sojourner Truth, a former slave, was a charismatic speaker who argued for equal rights for both black and white women.

ELIZABETH CADY STANTON

FOUGHT FOR WOMEN'S FULL EQUALITY WITH MEN

Elizabeth Cady Stanton was born on November 12, 1815, in Johnstown, New York. As a girl, she became interested in the activities at her father's law office and overheard the stories of women who had lost their property and children under New York divorce laws.

When she was a young woman, Elizabeth was attracted to the growing antislavery movement, through which she met a number of important people in her life. One was Henry Brewster Stanton, whom she married in 1840. Another was Lucretia Mott, whom she met the same year. The two women shared a deep frustration with the limitations that society placed on women and agreed they would one day organize a women's rights convention.

Elizabeth Cady Stanton campaigned for more than the right to vote. She also wanted property rights, equal wages, and rights for married women.

Eight years later, in July 1848, Stanton and Mott finally met near Seneca Falls, where Stanton and her family lived. The two women and three others, including Mott's sister, Martha Coffin Wright, decided to hold a women's rights convention in Seneca Falls later that month, on July 19 and 20. Stanton wrote the final draft of the Declaration of Sentiments. Modeled after the Declaration of Independence, it outlined eighteen offenses against women's rights, including their inability to vote.

Stanton was the most radical thinker of the convention's organizers. Despite her colleagues' concerns that the time was not yet right, she proposed a resolution in support of women's suffrage—the first public demand by American women for the vote. It was adopted by the approximately three hundred people who attended the convention at Seneca Falls.

In 1851, Stanton met Susan B. Anthony, whose talents and lifestyle seemed to complement her own. Anthony was a good organizer and a tireless campaigner. She was unmarried and free to travel, unlike Stanton, who had seven children to look after. Stanton was a more eloquent and persuasive writer, and she wrote many speeches for Anthony to deliver. Before the Civil War, Stanton worked mainly in New York State, where she and Anthony organized national and state women's rights conventions. She also campaigned for women's right to control their own property and helped to bring about a property law more favorable to women in 1860.

After the Civil War, Stanton and Anthony refused to support the Fifteenth Amendment, which gave African American men the right to vote but made no mention of women. This decision brought criticism from their antislavery friends and many suffrage leaders. Stanton and Anthony's response was to form, in 1869, an independent organization of like-minded women called the National Woman Suffrage Association (NWSA).

Stanton was president of NWSA for the entire twenty-one years of its existence. She focused on a range of women's issues, such as a married woman's right to keep her wages and a working woman's right to earn as much as male workers, but suffrage was her main concern. In 1878, she persuaded Senator Aaron Sargent from California to introduce a women's suffrage amendment to Congress. It did not pass, but it was reintroduced every year until Congress finally approved it in 1919 as the Nineteenth Amendment.

Stanton remained an advocate for women's rights until the end of her life. When NWSA merged with its rival sister organization in 1890 to become the National American Woman Suffrage Association (NAWSA), she again became president. Five years later her new *Woman's Bible* was published. A feminist reinterpretation of the Bible; the work shocked some Americans, including suffragists. After Stanton's death on October 26, 1902, her daughter Harriot Stanton Blatch continued the fight for suffrage that Stanton had helped to launch.

LUCY STONE

Lucy Stone was born on August 13, 1818, on her family's farm near West Brookfield, Massachusetts. Independent from the time she was a child, she attended college despite her father's objections. When she graduated from Oberlin College in Ohio in 1847, she became the first woman in Massachusetts to earn a college degree.

Drawn almost immediately into the lecture circuit, Stone began to give public speeches in support of women's rights and also against slavery. She attracted large audiences with her crystal-clear, musical voice. Although small, she was exceptionally courageous and diplomatic in the face of hostile crowds. One of the many people she won over to the suffrage cause was Susan B. Anthony, who heard Stone address a national women's rights convention that Stone helped organize in Worcester, Massachusetts, in 1850.

Opposite: A gifted speaker, Lucy Stone (left) inspired Susan B. Anthony to join the suffrage cause. Above: Stone graduated from Oberlin College in Ohio.

When the women's suffrage movement split in two in 1869, Stone helped establish the American Woman Suffrage Association (AWSA) and became the editor of its journal. Under Stone's editorship, AWSA's publication, called the *Woman's Journal*, persuaded its many, well-educated female readers that women's suffrage was consistent with American ideals. Known for good writing from respected contributors, the journal became known as the voice of the suffrage movement.

Stone's daughter, Alice, helped the two suffrage organizations reunite in 1890. Stone chaired the executive committee of their newly formed NAWSA. She died on October 18, 1893.

SUSAN B. ANTHONY

SYMBOL OF THE WOMEN'S RIGHTS MOVEMENT

Born on February 15, 1820, near Adams, Massachusetts, Susan B. Anthony grew up in a family that respected women. Her father, Daniel, was a Quaker, and he subscribed to the Quaker belief that in God's eyes, men and women are equals. In 1848, when Elizabeth Cady Stanton organized the first convention for women's rights in Seneca Falls, New York, Anthony's parents and sister attended, though she did not go herself.

Anthony met Stanton two years after that historic convention. The two women became friends, and they began to work as a team. Anthony was a great organizer, but she was not a gifted writer. Stanton, on the other hand, wrote powerful speeches, but she had seven children at home and needed someone like Anthony to deliver them.

The Civil War slowed the suffrage movement, but afterward, Anthony returned to the suffrage issue with renewed enthusiasm. In 1866, she presented Congress with petitions signed by thousands of Americans in favor of women's suffrage. Three years later, suffrage leaders debated whether to support the Fifteenth Amendment to the Constitution, which gave black men the vote. Anthony objected to giving black men the right to vote without giving it to women. She and Stanton established a new organization, the National Woman Suffrage Association (NWSA), which reflected their views.

For the next twenty-one years, Anthony helped lead NWSA and worked tirelessly to promote suffrage. She traveled to states where voters were deciding whether to give women the vote, and she lobbied Congress for an amendment to the Constitution. Although much of her organizational work was routine, Anthony revealed a flair for drama. She urged women to vote in the 1872 presidential election. After she and fourteen other women in her district managed to cast their ballots, they made newspaper headlines, and Anthony was arrested. At the nation's centennial celebration on July 4, 1876, Anthony was once again in the spotlight. During a reading of the Declaration of Independence in Philadelphia's Independence Hall, she interrupted the solemn proceedings to distribute copies of a "Declaration of Woman's Rights" written by Stanton.

Two years later, Senator Aaron Sargent from California proposed a women's suffrage amendment to the Constitution. Although Congress voted down the amendment, Anthony made sure it was reintroduced every year. Her annual appearance in Washington, D.C., helped make her a symbol of the suffrage movement.

Anthony was seventy years old when, in 1890, the two opposing camps of the suffrage movement finally united under one organization, the National American

Susan B. Anthony approached Congress annually to support a suffrage amendment and became a symbol of the women's rights movement.

Woman Suffrage Association (NAWSA). For most of the following decade she was president of the organization. Younger generations referred to her affectionately as "Aunt Susan" and were happy to follow her lead. She had become a legend.

Although Anthony officially retired from NAWSA in 1900, she stayed in close touch with the organization. She died on March 3, 1906.

FRANCES WILLARD

BROUGHT CONSERVATIVE WOMEN INTO THE SUFFRAGE MOVEMENT

Born on September 28, 1839, Frances Willard grew up on the family farm in Wisconsin Territory with her brother and sister. When she was seventeen, Frances became very upset that her brother could vote in a presidential election but she could not.

As a young woman, Willard worked in education, first as a teacher, and eventually, at the age of thirty-one, as president of a Methodist college for women. Then, in the mid-1870s, Willard became involved in the temperance movement. An increasing number of Americans believed that alcoholism threatened the well-being of families, and they tried to get everyone to stop drinking. Willard decided that the temperance movement was a perfect vehicle for achieving some improvements in women's lives, including the right to vote, which was most important to her.

Willard soon became active in the Women's Christian Temperance Union (WCTU), and within just a few years, she managed to change the direction of that powerful organization completely. At first, WCTU's members wanted to focus exclusively on temperance. Then Willard introduced the theme of home protection. Women had to vote, she pointed out, so they could protect their homes and society against bad influences, including alcoholic beverages. With her clever argument, Willard won over enough members to get herself elected president of the WCTU in 1879.

Under Frances Willard's dynamic leadership, which lasted for nineteen years, WCTU became an important ally of the suffrage movement. In 1880, the organization officially supported women's voting rights. As a result, thousands of its members decided to support that cause. Suffrage leaders such as Susan B. Anthony could not easily reach these conservative women, and they were grateful for Willard's help.

Frances Willard was, according to one historian, one of the most capable leaders of the nineteenth century. As president, she transformed WCTU into the largest women's organization of its time, with a membership of two hundred thousand women. She died on February 18, 1898, while still in office.

As president of the Women's Christian Temperance Union, Frances Willard encouraged her conservative membership to support the suffrage movement.

Anna Howard Shaw, pictured here as she drives in a parade, led the National American Woman Suffrage Association in the early 1900s.

ANNA HOWARD SHAW

ELOQUENT SPEAKER ADVANCED THE SUFFRAGE MOVEMENT

Anna Howard Shaw was born in Newcastle upon Tyne, England, on February 14, 1847. When she was four years old, her family moved to the United States, and her father soon took up a land claim on the frontier in Michigan. In the course of her lonely childhood, Anna learned to be resourceful and work very hard.

It took Shaw a few years to figure out her true calling. First she tried the ministry, and then the field of medicine. Almost immediately after she received her medical degree in 1886, however, Shaw came to the conclusion that she wanted to help disadvantaged women. The best way, she decided, was to win them the vote.

Shaw was an unusually good speaker, and in the late 1880s she went on lecture tours for her two favorite causes: suffrage and temperance. When the new NAWSA was formed in 1890, she was appointed the national lecturer.

Shaw worked for

This drawing depicts Shaw in her official role as the national lecturer for NAWSA.

NAWSA for twenty-five years, and in that time her greatest contribution was at the lecture podium. She spoke about women's suffrage at national conventions and before committees in Congress, and she lent her support to state campaigns for suffrage. She captivated audiences in every state of the Union and became one of the most eloquent speakers of the suffrage movement during her time.

In 1904, Shaw became president of NAWSA and held that position for eleven years. Her abilities as a leader did not match her gifts as an orator, and the organization was in a state of turmoil when she left. She continued to speak out for suffrage as the struggle for the vote neared its end. Shaw died on July 2, 1919.

Born on January 17, 1853, to a wealthy family, Alva Smith spent her childhood in Mobile, Alabama, and then, after the Civil War, in France. When she returned to the United States in the early 1870s, she was ready to conquer New York's high society—the wealthiest, and often the most powerful, residents of the city.

Alva's marriage in 1875 to William Kissam Vanderbilt, heir to a great fortune, was the event of the social season. By 1896 she was divorced, and the next year she married Oliver Belmont, another wealthy man. After her second husband's death in 1908, Alva Belmont made the remarkable transformation from socialite into suffragist.

Inspired by Anna Howard Shaw, the president of NAWSA, Belmont decided to devote her time and money to helping women win the vote. She rented a large space in New York City for NAWSA's headquarters and marched in suffrage parades shoulder to shoulder with women factory workers. Belmont was living proof that suffrage was an issue that concerned women of all social classes.

Messengers (above) and socialites like Alva Belmont (opposite) worked side by side in the suffrage movement.

When the suffragist leader Alice Paul left NAWSA to begin a new group and use more aggressive tactics, Belmont followed and became a member of its executive board. In 1921, after the women's suffrage amendment was finally ratified, she was elected president of Paul's National Woman's Party. She had donated $146,000—a fortune in those days—toward the purchase of a building for the party.

Belmont remained interested in women's rights issues for the rest of her life. She died in Paris, where she owned a house, on January 26, 1933.

HARRIOT STANTON BLATCH

BROUGHT WORKING-CLASS WOMEN INTO THE MOVEMENT

Harriot Stanton Blatch grew up in the center of the women's suffrage movement. Her mother, Elizabeth Cady Stanton, was one of the organizers of the historic women's rights convention in Seneca Falls, New York, where Harriot was born eight years later, on January 20, 1856. Harriot graduated from Vassar College in 1878 and moved to England with her British husband four years later.

When Blatch returned to New York State with her husband and daughter in 1902, she found the women's suffrage movement in the doldrums. Blatch thought she could rejuvenate movement by recruiting women laborers, who had been ignored by most suffrage leaders. In 1907 she established the Equality League of Self-Supporting Women, which eventually attracted almost twenty thousand women workers. Blatch's league members used some bold new tactics that eventually inspired organizations in other states:

Harriot Stanton Blatch, daughter of Elizabeth Cady Stanton, drew working-class women to the suffrage cause and thus revived the movement.

After Blatch and other New York suffragists lobbied the state legislature, New York became the first eastern state to ratify a women's suffrage amendment.

They held some of their meetings outside, where they attracted more attention, and they launched the first suffrage parades. Blatch also used her organization to lobby the legislators of New York State for a suffrage amendment. In 1913, thanks in large measure to Blatch's efforts, the New York legislature voted in favor of a women's suffrage amendment for the state. It was ratified in 1917, which made New York the first state in the East to give women the vote.

That same year, when the United States entered World War I, Blatch worked to support the war effort. After the end of the war and the ratification of the women's suffrage amendment, she worked in support of the federal Equal Rights Amendment. Blatch was also dedicated to other liberal causes, such as the establishment of the League of Nations, in the hopes of achieving world peace. She died on November 20, 1940.

Carrie Chapman Catt's independent spirit was nourished on the western frontier. Born Carrie Lane on January 9, 1859, she grew up on farms in Wisconsin and Iowa. Determined to go to college, she paid her own way through Iowa State College and graduated in 1880.

After the sudden death of her young husband, Leo Chapman, in 1886, Carrie began to work in the suffrage movement. By 1890, she was so passionate about the cause that her second husband, George William Catt, had to agree she could work for women's suffrage four months out of the year before she would marry him.

Catt focused on the state-by-state passage of suffrage.

Catt's talents and energy quickly became obvious to the leaders of NAWSA, including its president, Susan B. Anthony. In 1895, Catt set up and ran a committee to organize the women who were making speeches and talking to voters around the country. When Anthony retired as president of NAWSA in 1900, she asked Catt to be the new president.

In a short period of time, Catt rebuilt NAWSA into an organization that functioned much more efficiently. She resigned from her role as president in 1904 to care for her dying husband. When she returned to leadership in 1915, she created what became known as NAWSA's winning plan.

Catt decided that NAWSA should work on increasing the number of "suffrage states" where women could already vote, which totaled ten. New suffrage states would, she thought, increase pressure on Congress to pass an amendment. At the same time, NAWSA continued to campaign in Washington, D.C., for an amendment to the Constitution.

By this time, the nation had entered World War I. Even though Catt was a pacifist and opposed the war, she encouraged women to support the country's war effort because she thought their patriotism would impress voters. By 1917, Catt had helped to convince one very important voter to support women's suffrage: President Woodrow Wilson.

After Congress finally approved the Nineteenth Amendment in June 1919, Catt led a hard campaign for ratification that lasted fourteen long months. On August 18, 1920, the Tennessee legislature cast the last vote that was needed for the Nineteenth Amendment to become law.

Carrie Chapman Catt, pictured, encouraged suffragists to show patriotism through their support of U.S. involvement in World War I.

Shortly before women won the vote, Catt founded an organization to help women become educated voters. Called the National League of Women Voters, it continues to play an important role in American politics. Catt did not work in the organization herself, however. She spent the last decades of her life working for peace. She died on March 9, 1947.

Opposite: In 1916, Jeannette Rankin became the first woman elected to Congress and soon broadened support for the suffrage campaign. Above: Rankin addressed Congress about the need for a national women's suffrage amendment.

Born on the Montana frontier on June 11, 1880, Jeannette Rankin grew into an independent young woman. She began to work in the women's suffrage campaign when she was a student at the University of Washington in 1910.

Two years later, Rankin helped persuade Montana's legislators to approve a women's suffrage amendment to the state's constitution and put it before the voters. In October 1914, one month before the amendment went to the voters, Rankin spoke all over the state in support of women's suffrage: on courthouse steps, in front of country stores, and at mining camps. Montana gave women the vote on November 3.

Rankin decided that the best place to continue the fight for women's voting rights was as a member of Congress. In 1916, the popular suffragist ran on the Republican ticket for one of Montana's two congressmen-at-large seats in the House of Representatives. On November 7, 1916, she became the first woman elected to serve in Congress.

In Washington, D.C., Rankin pushed for a national women's suffrage amendment and championed women's rights. To her fellow congressmen she was a physical reminder of the many women in the country who still could not vote.

There was one other cause to which Rankin was very dedicated: She was a pacifist. She believed war was almost never a good idea. Soon after she joined Congress, she voted against sending American troops to fight in World War I. The next time she won a seat in Congress, in 1940, she was the only one to vote against sending troops into World War II, which made her a very unpopular figure. By the time Rankin died on May 18, 1973, however, she had become a legend in the eyes of a new generation of women's rights leaders.

Rankin's groundbreaking political position allowed her to fight directly for women's rights.

ALICE PAUL

WROTE THE EQUAL RIGHTS AMENDMENT

Born on January 11, 1885, Alice Paul grew up in Mooresville, New Jersey, a small Quaker community near Philadelphia, Pennsylvania. Her family lived according to the Quaker belief that men and women were equal. Alice was encouraged to graduate from Swarthmore College and later receive advanced degrees in social work.

Alice Paul had a a talent for getting maximum public attention for her suffrage work. When she and a small group of women from NAWSA organized a suffrage parade in Washington, D.C., Paul chose March 3, 1913, the day before President Woodrow Wilson's inauguration. Five thousand women marched down Pennsylvania Avenue, and huge crowds of Washingtonians and out-of-town visitors gathered around them.

Four years later, Paul organized members of the National Woman's Party, which she had helped establish, to hold up picket signs in favor of women's suffrage in front of the White House. After 168 people, including Paul, were arrested for blocking the sidewalk, she went on a hunger strike.

The activities of Paul and and her colleagues offended many Americans, but historians agree that all the attention they received actually benefited the cause of women's suffrage for a number of reasons. After a period in which little progress had been made, people began to think and talk about the issue once again. Since President Wilson did not like the tactics of the National Woman's Party, he could not help comparing them with the much more moderate behavior of Carrie Catt and NAWSA, which Paul had left years earlier. The comparison made NAWSA seem reasonable, and Wilson asked Congress to pass the Nineteenth Amendment to the Constitution giving women the vote.

In 1923, three years after the women's suffrage amendment was passed, Paul wrote and introduced the Equal Rights Amendment. This amendment to the Constitution said men and women would be treated equally under the law. She worked for that amendment for almost fifty years and lived to see it approved by Congress in 1972, though it was never ratified by the states. Alice Paul died on July 9, 1977.

Alice Paul, a founder of the National Woman's Party and author of the Equal Rights Amendment, used dramatic new tactics to bring public attention to the movement.

CHRONOLOGY

January 1648	Margaret Brent demands two votes in the colony of Maryland's assembly.
1792	Mary Wollstonecraft's *The Vindication of the Rights of Woman* is published.
1838	In a series of letters published as a pamphlet, Angelina Grimké defends her right to speak out anywhere for abolitionism.
July 19–20, 1848	Three hundred people attend the women's rights convention in Seneca Falls, where a resolution is passed demanding women's suffrage.
1851	Sojourner Truth gives her famous "Ain't I a Woman?" speech in Akron, Ohio.
1866	Susan B. Anthony presents Congress with petitions signed by thousands of Americans asking for the vote for women.
1869	The growing women's suffrage movement splits into two groups: the National Woman Suffrage Association, led by Elizabeth Cady Stanton and Susan B. Anthony, and the American Woman Suffrage Association, led by Lucy Stone and others; the territory of Wyoming is the first territory or state to give women the right to vote in any election.
November 5, 1872	Susan B. Anthony votes in a presidential election, for which she is arrested.
1880	The Women's Christian Temperance Union, under the leadership of Frances Willard, decides to support women's suffrage.
1890	The two main suffrage organizations reunite to form the National American Woman Suffrage Association, led by Elizabeth Cady Stanton and Susan B. Anthony.
1907	Harriot Stanton Blatch organizes the Equality League of Self-Supporting Women and attracts thousands of factory workers and other working women to the suffrage movement.

The dedication of suffragists led to the ratification of the Nineteenth Amendment and inspires women's rights activists to this day.

March 3, 1913	Organized by Alice Paul, five thousand women march down Pennsylvania Avenue in Washington, D.C., to demand the right to vote.
1915	Carrie Chapman Catt becomes president of the National American Woman Suffrage Association and puts together her "winning plan."
November 7, 1916	Jeannette Rankin is the first woman elected to serve in Congress.
June 1919	Congress approves the Nineteenth Amendment to the Constitution, which gives every female citizen of the United States of voting age the right to vote.
August 18, 1920	The Nineteenth Amendment is ratified by the states.

FOR FURTHER INFORMATION

BOOKS

Colleen Adams, *Women's Suffrage: A Primary Source History of the Women's Rights Movement in America.* New York: Rosen Central Primary Source, 2003.

Jules Archer, *Breaking Barriers: The Feminist Revolution from Susan B. Anthony to Margaret Sanger to Betty Friedan.* New York: Penguin Putnam, 1996.

Lydia D. Bjornlund, *Women of the Suffrage Movement.* San Diego, CA: Lucent, 2002.

Lisa Frederkisen Bohannen, *Failure Is Impossible: The Story of Susan B. Anthony.* Greensboro, NC: Morgan Reynolds, 2001.

Kristina Dumbeck, *Leaders of Women's Suffrage.* San Diego, CA: Lucent, 2001

Martha Keenall, *Susan B. Anthony: Voice for Women's Voting Rights.* Springfield, NJ: Enslow, 1997.

Kathryn Lasky, *A Time for Courage: The Suffragette Diary of Kathleen Bowen.* New York: Scholastic, 2002.

Barbara A. Somerville, *Votes for Women! The Story of Carrie Chapman Catt.* Greensboro, NC: Morgan Reynolds, 2002.

WEBSITES

National Women's Hall of Fame
www.greatwomen.org
Look up the biographies of suffragists and other important women at the website of the National Women's Hall of Fame.

National Women's History Museum
www.nmwh.org
The National Women's History Museum offers a virtual tour of its collection of buttons, banners, and ribbons from the women's suffrage movement.

ABOUT THE AUTHOR

Deborah Kops has written nine other nonfiction books for children, including a biography of Zachary Taylor. Her work has appeared in many newspapers and magazines, among them *the New York Times*, *Boston Globe*, *Vermont Life*, and *Country Journal*. Ms. Kops graduated from the University of Michigan and holds a master's degree in education from Antioch-Putney graduate school. She lives with her husband and son in the Greater Boston area.